A Note to Parents

DK READERS is a compellin beginning readers, designed leading literacy experts, incl Director of the School of Edu University. Dr. Gambrell has served on the Board of Directors of the International Reading Association and as President of the National Reading Conference.

Beautiful illustrations and superb full-color photographs combine with engaging, easy-to-read stories to offer a fresh approach to each subject in the series. Each DK READER is guaranteed to capture a child's interest while developing his or her reading skills, general knowledge, and love of reading.

The five levels of DK READERS are aimed at different reading abilities, enabling you to choose the books that are exactly right for your child:

Pre-level 1: Learning to read
Level 1: Beginning to read
Level 2: Beginning to read alone
Level 3: Reading alone
Level 4: Proficient readers

The "normal" age at which a child begins to read can be anywhere from three to eight years old, so these levels are intended only as a general guideline.

No matter which level you select, you can be sure that you are helping your child learn to read, then read to learn!

LONDON, NEW YORK, MUNICH,
MELBOURNE, AND DELHI

Senior Editor Linda Esposito
Senior Art Editor Andrew Burgess
Managing Art Editor Peter Bailey
US Editor Regina Kahney
Production Josie Alabaster
Photography John Daniels
Jacket Designer Chris Drew

Reading Consultant
Linda B. Gambrell, Ph.D.

First American Edition, 1999
05 10 9 8 7 6
Published in the United States by DK Publishing, Inc.
375 Hudson Street, New York, New York 10014

Published in Great Britain by Dorling Kindersley Limited.

Library of Congress Cataloging-in-Publication Data
Wallace, Karen
    Duckling Days / written by Karen Wallace.
       p.   cm. -- (Dorling Kindersley readers. Level 1)
      Summary: A mother duck builds her nest, lays her eggs, hatches
six ducklings, and teaches them about life on their own.
    ISBN 0-7894-3994-8 (pb) -- ISBN 0-7894-3995-6 (hc)
      1. Ducks--Infancy--Juvenile literature. [1. Ducks.
2. Animals--Infancy.] I. Title. II. Series.
    QL696.A52W33 1999
    598.4'1139--dc21
                                   98-41846
                                     CIP
                                     AC

Color reproduction by Colourscan, Singapore
Printed and bound in China by L Rex Printing Co., Ltd.

The publisher would like to thank the following for
their kind permission to reproduce their photographs:
Key: t=top, b=below, l=left, r=right, c=center

Barrie Watts:
5cr, 6b, 7tr, 26cl (below), 26cl, 27c (below),
27r, 28cl (above)
All other images © Dorling Kindersley.
For further information see www.dkimages.com

Discover more at

www.dk.com

DK READERS

BEGINNING TO READ **1**

Duckling Days

Written by Karen Wallace

DK Publishing, Inc.

In the grass
beside the river
a mother duck
builds her nest.

She gathers grass and
makes a hollow.

She lines her nest with
downy feathers.

nest

In a nest
beside the river
a mother duck
lays six white eggs.

egg

She keeps them warm
beneath her body.
Inside each egg
a duckling grows.

A duckling hatches
from his egg.

shell He cracks the shell.

He makes a hole
with his tiny beak.

He taps and pushes.

He breaks out of the shell
and squeezes out.

Other ducklings
hatch beside him.
At first their legs
are weak and wobbly.

Their downy feathers
are wet and sticky.
They dry out quickly
near their mother.

Mother duck has
six fluffy ducklings.
She leads them down
toward the river.

One little duckling
is left behind.

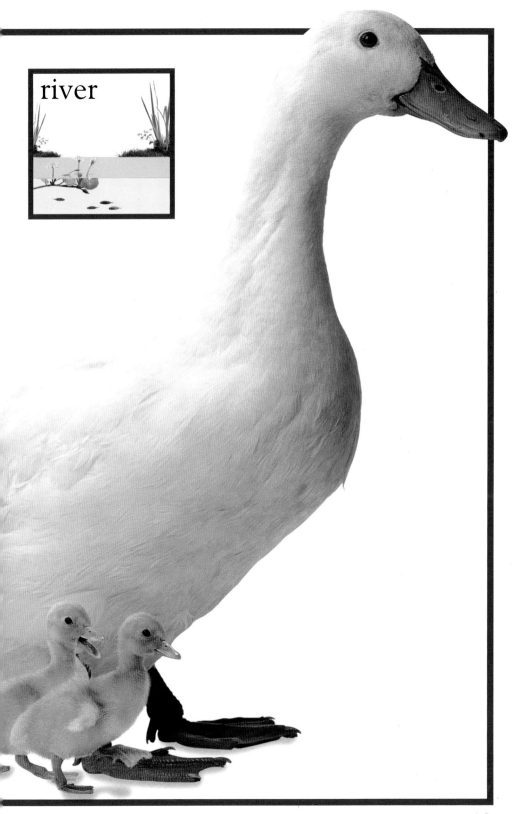

river

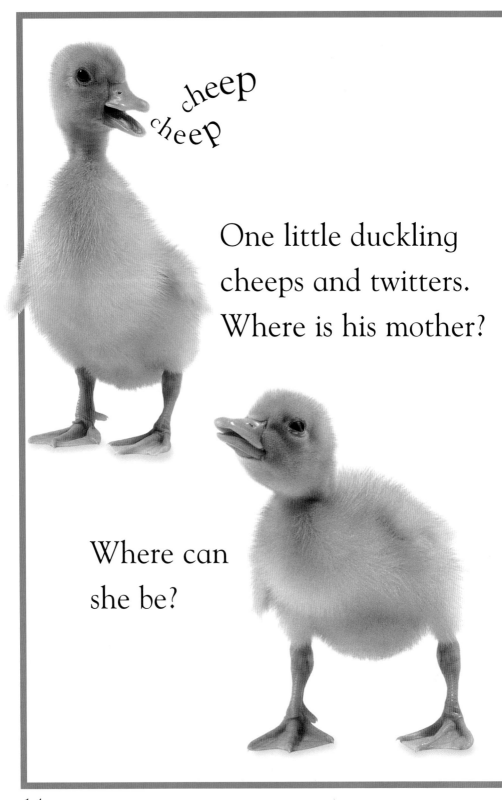

cheep
cheep

One little duckling
cheeps and twitters.
Where is his mother?

Where can
she be?

The little duckling
runs to find her.

cheep

He's afraid to be
on his own.

Five ducklings jump
into the water.
They push and paddle
with webbed feet.

webbed
feet

cheep

The little duckling
finds his family.

Mother duck checks
her ducklings.

Six fluffy babies
swim beside her.

In the river
the water is deep.
Mother duck dives
and leaves her ducklings.

She nibbles plants.
She chases beetles.

Six little ducklings
look around them.

Where is mother duck?
Where can she be?

cheep

cheep

cheep

Cheep! Cheep!
The ducklings call for mother.

cheep

cheep

cheep

A bee buzzes in the air.

A frog croaks from a lily pad.

croak

Two birds sing on a branch.

tweet tweet

But mother duck
does not answer.
Where has she gone?
Where can she be?

Quack! Quack!
She pops up in the water!

quack

quack

cheep

cheep

cheep

Cheep! Cheep!
Her ducklings huddle around her.

Next time
they will be braver.

cheep

cheep

cheep

The growing ducklings
snap at tadpoles.
They pull at pondweed
with their yellow bills.

bill

They like to dabble
in the water.

They watch their mother.
They do what she does.

The ducklings' down grows into feathers.

feathers

They watch their mother clean her feathers.

She flaps and fluffs.

She plucks and preens.

She strokes
and smooths.

Mother duck
is combed
and clean!

29

Five young ducks waddle
from the river.

They shake the water
from their backs.
They flap their wings
just like their mother.
They clean their feathers
with their beaks.

wing

One young duck
dabbles in the water.
He's happy being
on his own.

Picture Word List

nest

page 5

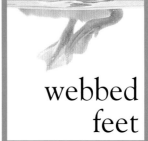
webbed
feet
page 16

egg

page 6

bill
page 26

shell
page 8

feathers
page 28

river

page 13

wing
page 30